The Acceptance and Commitment Therapy (ACT) Diary

A guide and companion for moving toward the things that matter in your life

2022

Dr Nic Hooper and Dr Freddy Jackson Brown

The Acceptance and Commitment Therapy (ACT) Diary 2022

Published by:
Pavilion Publishing and Media Ltd
Blue Sky Offices
Cecil Pashley Way
Shoreham by Sea
West Sussex
BN43 5FF
Tel: 01273 434 943
Fax: 01273 227 308
Email: info@pavpub.com

Published 2021

A catalogue record for this book is available from the British Library.

ISBN: 978-1-914010-83-5

Pavilion Publishing and Media is a leading publisher of books, training materials and digital content in mental health, social care and allied fields. Pavilion and its imprints offer must-have knowledge and innovative learning solutions underpinned by sound research and professional values.

Cover design: Phil Morash, Pavilion Publishing and Media Ltd.
Printing: Ashford Press

Contents

2022 Year Planner 6
Welcome to The Acceptance and Commitment Therapy (ACT) Diary 2022 8
How to Use This Diary 9
Week 1: What Do You Want? 12
Week 2: An Introduction to Values 16
Week 3: Value Domains 20
Week 4: Smart Goals 24
Week 5: Identifying Values 28
Week 6: Refining Values 34
Week 7: Domain 1: Friends and Social Relationships 38
Week 8: Managing our Thoughts and Feelings 42
Week 9: Domain 2: Work and Career 46
Week 10: What is Willingness? 52
Week 11: Domain 3: Family Relationships 56
Week 12: Exploring Willingness – The Unwelcome Guest 60
Week 13: Domain 4: Education and Learning 64
Week 14: What is Defusion? 68
Week 15: Domain 5: Intimate Relationships 74
Week 16: Exploring Defusion – Having the Thought 78
Week 17: Domain 6: Self-development and Growth 82
Week 18: What is Contact with the Present Moment? 86
Week 19: Domain 7: Recreation and Leisure 92
Week 20: Exploring Contact with the Present Moment – Breathing 96
Week 21: Domain 8: Spirituality 100
Week 22: What is the Observing Self? 104
Week 23: Domain 9: Community and Citizenship 110
Week 24: Exploring the Observing Self – The Sky and the Weather 114
Week 25: Domain 10: Health and Physical Wellbeing 118
Week 26: What is the Hexaflex? 122

Week 27: A Values Exercise – Writing a Eulogy 126
Week 28: Introducing Self-Compassion 132
Week 29: Exploring Self-Compassion – Helping a Child 136
Week 30: Personal Values Statement: Health 140
Week 31: Introducing Experiential Avoidance 144
Week 32: Personal Values Statement: Work 150
Week 33: Exploring Experiential Avoidance – The White Bear 154
Week 34: Personal Values Statement: Leisure 158
Week 35: Exploring Experiential Avoidance – A Crucial Side Effect 162
Week 36: Personal Values Statement: Relationships 166
Week 37: Exploring Experiential Avoidance – A Ball in the Water 172
Week 38: Giving You The Reins 176
Week 39: Exploring Willingness – Quicksand 180
Week 40: Exploring Willingness Further – Tug-of-War with a Monster 184
Week 41: Exploring Defusion – Leaves on a Stream 190
Week 42: Exploring Defusion Further – Hands as Thoughts 194
Week 43: Exploring Mindfulness – The Body Scan 198
Week 44: Exploring Mindfulness Further – Walking Aware 202
Week 45: Exploring the Observing Self – Description and Evaluation 208
Week 46: Exploring the Observing Self Further – Who is Noticing? 212
Week 47: Exploring Values – Your Heroes 216
Week 48: Exploring Committed Action – Waiting for the Wrong Train 220
Week 49: Bringing it all Together: Driving the Bus 224
Week 50: Bringing it all Together: Passenger Revolt! 230
Week 51: Bringing it all Together: Keep on Driving 234
Week 52: Ending the Year 238
Goal Bank 246
About Nic and Freddy 250

Personal Information

Name:

Address:

Home Phone Number:

Mobile Phone Number:

Email:

Office Phone Number:

Work Address:

If you find this diary please contact:

2022 Year Planner

	January	February	March	April	May	June
Sun					1	
Mon					2	
Tue		1	1		3	
Wed		2	2		4	1
Thu		3	3		5	2
Fri		4	4	1	6	3
Sat	1	5	5	2	7	4
Sun	2	6	6	3	8	5
Mon	3	7	7	4	9	6
Tue	4	8	8	5	10	7
Wed	5	9	9	6	11	8
Thu	6	10	10	7	12	9
Fri	7	11	11	8	13	10
Sat	8	12	12	9	14	11
Sun	9	13	13	10	15	12
Mon	10	14	14	11	16	13
Tue	11	15	15	12	17	14
Wed	12	16	16	13	18	15
Thu	13	17	17	14	19	16
Fri	14	18	18	15	20	17
Sat	15	19	19	16	21	18
Sun	16	20	20	17	22	19
Mon	17	21	21	18	23	20
Tue	18	22	22	19	24	21
Wed	19	23	23	20	25	22
Thu	20	24	24	21	26	23
Fri	21	25	25	22	27	24
Sat	22	26	26	23	28	25
Sun	23	27	27	24	29	26
Mon	24	28	28	25	30	27
Tue	25		29	26	31	28
Wed	26		30	27		29
Thu	27		31	28		30
Fri	28			29		
Sat	29			30		
Sun	30					
Mon	31					

2022 Year Planner

	July	August	September	October	November	December
Sun						
Mon		1				
Tue		2			1	
Wed		3			2	
Thu		4	1		3	1
Fri	1	5	2		4	2
Sat	2	6	3	1	5	3
Sun	3	7	4	2	6	4
Mon	4	8	5	3	7	5
Tue	5	9	6	4	8	6
Wed	6	10	7	5	9	7
Thu	7	11	8	6	10	8
Fri	8	12	9	7	11	9
Sat	9	13	10	8	12	10
Sun	10	14	11	9	13	11
Mon	11	15	12	10	14	12
Tue	12	16	13	11	15	13
Wed	13	17	14	12	16	14
Thu	14	18	15	13	17	15
Fri	15	19	16	14	18	16
Sat	16	20	17	15	19	17
Sun	17	21	18	16	20	18
Mon	18	22	19	17	21	19
Tue	19	23	20	18	22	20
Wed	20	24	21	19	23	21
Thu	21	25	22	20	24	22
Fri	22	26	23	21	25	23
Sat	23	27	24	22	26	24
Sun	24	28	25	23	27	25
Mon	25	29	26	24	28	26
Tue	26	30	27	25	29	27
Wed	27	31	28	26	30	28
Thu	28		29	27		29
Fri	29		30	28		30
Sat	30			29		31
Sun	31			30		
Mon				31		

Welcome to The Acceptance and Commitment Therapy (ACT) Diary 2022

The Acceptance and Commitment Therapy (ACT) Diary 2022 is designed to help you move toward the things that are important to you over the coming year. If this is the second, third, fourth or even fifth time that you are using our diary then you'll know what to expect. We do hope that focusing on your values will continue to positively impact your wellbeing.

The diary is based on an approach to human suffering called 'Acceptance and Commitment Therapy' or 'ACT'. However, don't let the word 'therapy' scare you off! Although there is no doubt that ACT is super useful for those who seek psychological support, its principles are relevant to everyone. ACT works to increase what is called psychological flexibility, and this is helpful regardless of whether or not someone has a formal diagnosis. In non-jargon terms, psychological flexibility means connecting fully with all of our experiences, including difficult thoughts and feelings, whilst doing things that are personally meaningful.

This is important because it is easy to become disconnected from our moment-by-moment experiences and from what really matters to us. In other words, our values. When this happens, and it happens to us all to varying degrees and at different times, everyday life can feel less meaningful and more of a chore. And conversely, when we do the things that matter to us, we tend to feel more fulfilled and in tune with life.

How to Use This Diary

This diary is very easy to use. Specifically, all you have to do is to read and engage with our weekly exercises and ideas.

When we say the word *'our'* we are referring to Dr Nic Hooper and Dr Freddy Jackson Brown. In fact, given that we will be spending so much time together it may be useful to imagine us like a couple of friends, speaking from the heart to get you doing the things that are important to you.

If you are interested, you can find out more about each of us at the back of this diary.

Space for general reflection

Throughout this diary we'll occasionally give you a page or two for general reflection. What you write here is up to you. You might want to think about how you're feeling, and what is contributing to you feeling that way. As you get further into the diary and the year, you could reflect on whether ACT, and a focus on values and goals in particular, is making a difference in your life.

We'll start each space for general reflection with the following broad pointers: "Use this space to record the ups and downs of the past few weeks. You may also want to write down what you have learned about yourself and the nature of life." These are based on what we ourselves use the section for, but they may not reflect what suits you best or what you choose to use it for.

You can start right away, on the facing page. Remember that there are no right and wrong answers. It's up to you to decide what to write – what you think might be valuable for you to set down now, and potentially helpful to look back on from further along your journey.

December 2021/January 2022

Use this space to record the ups and downs of the past few weeks. You may also want to write down what you have learned about yourself and the nature of life.

Week 1

Welcome to Week 1.

Let's get going with an activity based on a very simple question: What do you want?

Use the space on this page and opposite to list some of the things you'd like to achieve in the next few months. You could even think of these as your New Year's resolutions. At this point, don't worry about how big, small, possible or difficult these goals might be. Just list what pops into your head.

Once you have your list, choose a small goal, write it at the bottom of this page, and try to complete it over the next week. If you succeed, tick the box!

You can also write your goal in the summary box provided at the beginning of each weekly view (see next page for an example). This will help you keep in mind the things that you are striving to move towards and achieve.

Week 1

Summary goal for the week

27 Monday

28 Tuesday

29 Wednesday

January 2022 Week 1

Thursday

Friday

Saturday

Sunday

> *It's no use going back to yesterday, because I was a different person then.*
>
> *Lewis Carroll*

Week 2

Welcome to Week 2.

How did you get on? Did you complete the goal from Week 1? Please take a moment to reflect on your experience of this. For example, which goal did you choose to complete, why did you choose that goal, how did you feel if you completed the goal, and if you didn't complete the goal then what got in the way?

An Introduction to Values

Values are about how you want to behave, moment-by-moment, during your life. In some ways, they describe the sort of person you want to be. For example, if the value of *'caring'* is important to you then what can you do that reflects this value? How can you behave towards yourself, others and the environment in a caring way? People that live more in line with their values tend to be psychologically healthier. The thing most people say after we say those words is *'I don't even know what my values are'*. That is one thing this diary will help you with, as it is jam-packed with different ways of tuning into values.

We're going to start with a really simple exercise. We want you to imagine that you've won the lottery and below we'd like you to detail, in the left hand column, how you might spend your winnings. Leave the right-hand column blank for now. As an additional activity, please choose another goal from your Week 1 list, write it at the bottom of this page and try to complete it before we next speak.

January 2022 Week 2

Summary goal for the week

3 Monday

4 Tuesday

5 Wednesday

January 2022 Week 2

Thursday

Friday

Saturday

Sunday

Your values become your destiny.

Mahatma Gandhi

Week 3

Welcome to Week 3.

We asked you to do two things last week. Firstly, we asked you to complete another goal from the first list that you made in this diary. Did you manage to do it? As with Week 1, take a moment to reflect on your experience of trying (and maybe succeeding?) to do something important to you.

The other thing we asked you to do was to think about how you might spend lottery winnings. We'd like you to flick back to Week 2 and try to pin-point the possible values that are underneath your lottery spending (please write some of those values in the right hand column of that exercise). That is, once you get past the big houses and the fast cars, answers to the lottery question tend to reveal some important things in our lives. For example, *'self-care', 'travel'* or *'learning'* might be values underneath the words *'have lots of holidays'*. We'd now like you to write down a small goal that is in line with one of the values that the lottery question revealed, and try to complete it over the next week.

Value Domains

From completing the lottery question you may begin to see that values exist in different domains of our life. These domains may or may not be important. Consequently, we'd like you to complete the exercise below in order to determine which areas are important to you and how much you neglect them. In column 2 please rate the overall importance of the domain to you on a scale of 1-10. In column 3 please rate how much behavioural attention you tend to give to that domain, in other words the extent to which you put it into action. Finally, please subtract the smaller number from the larger to create a *'concern'* score for each domain in column 4. The higher the number, the larger the discrepancy between what is important to you and how much you are acting in line with it.

	Importance (1-10)	**Action (1-10)**	**Concern (1-10)**
Friends and Social Relationships			
Work and Career			
Family Relationships			
Education and Learning			
Intimate Relationships			
Self-development and Growth			
Recreation and Leisure			
Spirituality			
Community and Citizenship			
Physical Health and Well-being			

January 2022 — Week 3

Summary goal for the week

10 Monday

11 Tuesday

12 Wednesday

January 2022 Week 3

Thursday

Friday

Saturday

Sunday

Values are like fingerprints. Nobody's are the same, but you leave them all over everything you do.

Elvis Presley

Week 4

Welcome to Week 4.

Did you manage to complete the goal related to the lottery task? If so, what did you think and/or feel before, during and after you had completed the goal? If you did not complete the goal, what barriers (internal or external) stopped you?

Now look back to the domains exercise. Did you learn anything important? Which domain are you neglecting the most? In the space below we'd like you to record a goal that relates to the domain with the highest *'concern'* score and try to complete it over the next week.

SMART Goals

Each week thus far we have asked you to complete a goal. However, we have done this without giving you any information about the best way to set goals in the first place (which is pretty naughty of us!). When you set goals, try to make them SMART (Specific, Measurable, Achievable, Relevant and Timely).

Specific: This is about being as precise as possible with regards to what you want to achieve. The more specific your description, the easier it is to know if you achieved it.

Measurable: This is about setting goals you can measure so that you know when you have achieved them.

Achievable: Is your goal really achievable? Setting goals that are unrealistic or a long way in the future makes life difficult. If you have a large goal, then it's better to break it down into smaller steps.

Relevant: This is about checking that the goal really reflects your underlying values. It is quite common to set goals that we think we *'should'* do, but deep down we may not really care about them.

Timely: This is about being clear when you will complete your goal. It is important to be precise about this.

Example of a SMART goal:

S My goal is to lose weight (specific).

M I will aim for 2 kg and I will exercise 3 times a week (measurable).

A 2kg is attainable based on my experience (achievable).

R This is important to me because I value being healthy (relevant).

T I will complete this goal within 2 months (timely).

January 2022 Week 4

Summary goal for the week

17 Monday

18 Tuesday

19 Wednesday

Thursday

Friday

Saturday

Sunday

You are never too old to set another goal or to dream a new dream.

C.S. Lewis

Week 5

Welcome to Week 5.

Did you manage to complete the goal related to the *'concern'* domain? If so, what did you think and/or feel before, during and after you had completed the goal? If not, what barriers (internal or external) stopped you? And did you make the goal SMART? If so, then great! If not, then remember to be as precise as possible when setting your goals.

Note: At the back of this diary you'll find a 'Goal Bank' where you can save any goals you don't manage to complete. Then you'll be able to return to those goals at some point in the future.

Ok, thus far you have had a gentle introduction to the concepts of goals and values but now we are going to start digging a little more! On the next page is a list of common values. We'd like you to cross out boxes until you have the three most important left (do this with a pencil so that you can use the values list as a reference point throughout the year). Then in the space below we'd like you to write down a goal that would bring one of those three values to life over the next week.

Identifying Values

Having a life filled with novelty and change	Teaching others	Being at one with God	Being wealthy	Showing respect to parents and elders	Helping others
Maintaining the safety and security of my loved ones	Meeting my obligations	Being physically fit	Eating healthy food	Acting consistently with my religious beliefs	Being loyal to friends and family
Having a life filled with adventure	Being admired by many people	Making sure to repay favours and not be indebted to people	Having an exciting life	Being curious, discovering new things	Being safe from danger
Figuring things out, solving problems	Being self disciplined and resisting temptation	Engaging in sporting activities	Showing respect for tradition	Connecting with nature	Creating beauty (in any domain)
Building and repairing things	Promoting justice and caring for the weak	Being sexually desirable	Caring for others	Having a sense of accomplish-ment and making a lasting contribution	Striving to be a better person
Being competent and effective	Having influence over people	Accepting others as they are	Being honest	Having relationships involving love and affection	Enjoying music, art or drama
Researching things	Engaging in clearly defined work	Working with my hands	Being in charge	Being ambitious and hardworking	Acting with courage
Designing things	Competing with others	Being self sufficient	Being creative	Organising things	Gaining wisdom

January 2022 Week 5

Summary goal for the week

24 Monday

25 Tuesday

26 Wednesday

January 2022 Week 5

Thursday

Friday

Saturday

Sunday

"You have brains in your head. You have feet in your shoes. You can steer yourself any direction you choose."

Dr Seuss

Space for general reflection

Use this space to record the ups and downs of the past few weeks. You may also want to write down what you have learned about yourself and the nature of life.

Week 6

Welcome to Week 6.

How did you get on? Did you manage to complete a goal related to the values list exercise from Week 5? If so, what did you think and/or feel before, during and after you had completed the goal? If you did not complete the goal, what barriers (internal or external) stopped you?

Sometimes the exercise from Week 5 by itself isn't enough to give people a sense of which values are important to them. Consequently, on the next page there is another values sorting exercise that we'd like you to complete. As with Week 5, we'd like you to cross out boxes until you have the three most important left (do this in pencil so you can use the values list as a reference point throughout the year). Then in the space below we'd like you to write down a goal that would bring one of those three values to life over the next week.

Refining Values

Acceptance	Fairness	Order
Adventure	Fitness	Open-mindedness
Assertiveness	Flexibility	Patience
Authenticity	Friendliness	Persistence
Beauty	Forgiveness	Respect
Caring	Fun	Responsibility
Challenge	Generosity	Romance
Compassion	Gratitude	Self-care
Connection	Honesty	Self-development
Contribution	Humour	Sensuality
Courage	Humility	Spirituality
Creativity	Independence	Supportiveness
Curiosity	Intimacy	Trust
Encouragement	Justice	Write your own
Equality	Kindness	Write your own
Excitement	Love	Write your own

January/February 2022 Week 6

Summary goal for the week

31 Monday

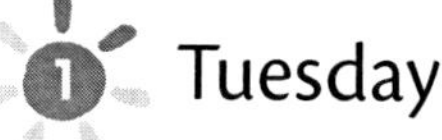

1 Tuesday

2 Wednesday

February 2022 Week 6

Thursday

Friday

Saturday

Sunday

> *The world is more malleable than you think and it's waiting for you to hammer it into shape.*
>
> *Bono*

Week 7

Welcome to Week 7.

How did you get on? Did you manage to complete a goal related to the values list exercise from Week 6? If so, what did you think and/or feel before, during and after you had completed the goal? If you did not complete the goal, what barriers (internal or external) stopped you?

Up to this point we have asked you to think about value domains and the different values that might be important to you. However, the interesting thing about values is that they can change depending on the domain. Consequently, in the coming weeks we are going to delve a little deeper again. Specifically, across each value domain we are going to ask you to write down (and complete) both a small and a bold goal. As a reminder, the value domains we identified in Week 5 were:

- Domain 1: Friends and Social Relationships
- Domain 2: Work and Career
- Domain 3: Family Relationships
- Domain 4: Education and Learning
- Domain 5: Intimate Relationships
- Domain 6: Self-development and Growth
- Domain 7: Recreation and Leisure
- Domain 8: Spirituality
- Domain 9: Community and Citizenship
- Domain 10: Health and Physical Wellbeing

Domain 1: Friends and Social Relationships

From the values lists in Week 5 and Week 6, which value would you like to bring to life in the domain of *friends and social relationships*?

Please write a very small commitment, which aligns with this value, and is in this domain, to be completed over the next week.

Now please write a bold commitment, which aligns with this value, and is in this domain, to be completed over the next two weeks.

Please make a note of the barriers (both internal and external) that you think might stop you from completing these goals.

February 2022 Week 7

Summary goal for the week

7 Monday

8 Tuesday

9 Wednesday

February 2022 Week 7

Thursday

Friday

Saturday

Sunday

"To get the full value of joy you must have someone to divide it with."

Mark Twain

Week 8

Welcome to Week 8.

How did you get on? Did you complete the small goal from the *friends and social relationships* domain? Please take a moment to reflect on your experience. For example, which goal did you choose to complete, why did you choose this goal, how did you feel if you completed the goal, and if you didn't manage to complete the goal then what got in the way?

If you haven't already done so then in the next week please try to complete the bold goal from the *friends and social relationships* domain. If you have already completed both the small and bold goals from Week 7 (or if it isn't appropriate to complete the bold goal this week), then please use the space below to write a couple more goals for this domain to complete over the next week.

Managing our Thoughts and Feelings

You will notice that we keep asking you to think about barriers. The reason for this is because people often let their own thoughts and feelings (internal barriers) stop them from doing things that are important. The more we understand these barriers, the more we are able to notice and overcome them. For example, once we are aware of how our thoughts and feelings are interfering with us doing the things that matter, then we can use some of ACT's core processes to manage them. These processes, which we will explore in the coming weeks, are:

Willingness: We humans try our utmost to avoid negative and uncomfortable thoughts and feelings. However, if we can learn to take them along for the ride, then we will be freer to engage in action.

Defusion: We humans tend to be very attached to our own thoughts. However, if we can distance ourselves from them, and hold them lightly, then we will better be able to do the things that are important to us.

Contact with the present moment: We humans can spend a lot of time ruminating about the past or worrying about the future. However, by contacting the present moment we will be able to appreciate the beauty and opportunity that surrounds us in the now.

Observing self: We humans build stories about who we are that can serve to restrict us. However, if we can instead observe our stories, then we will be less imprisoned by them.

Summary goal for the week

14 Monday

15 Tuesday

16 Wednesday

February 2022 Week 8

Thursday

Friday

Saturday

Sunday

The soul becomes dyed with the colour of its thoughts.

Marcus Aurelius

Week 9

Welcome to Week 9.

How did you get on? Did you complete the bold goal (or an alternative goal) from the *friends and social relationships* domain? Please take a moment to reflect on your experience. For example, which goal did you choose to complete, why did you choose this goal, how did you feel if you completed the goal, and if you didn't manage to complete the goal then what got in the way?

Domain 2: Work and Career

From the values lists in Week 5 and Week 6, which value would you like to bring to life in the domain of *work and career*?

Please write a very small commitment, which aligns with this value, and is in this domain, to be completed over the next week.

Now please write a bold commitment, which aligns with this value, and is in this domain, to be completed over the next two weeks.

Please make a note of the barriers (both internal and external) that you think might stop you from completing these goals.

February 2022

Week 9

Summary goal for the week

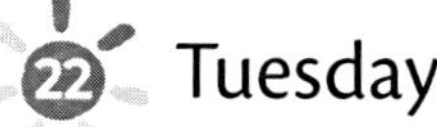

Monday

Tuesday

Wednesday

February 2022 Week 9

I think you should take your job seriously, but not yourself – that is the best combination.

Judi Dench

Space for general reflection

Use this space to record the ups and downs of the past few weeks. You may also want to write down what you have learned about yourself and the nature of life.

Week 10

Welcome to Week 10.

How did you get on? Did you complete the small goal from the *work and career* domain? Please take a moment to reflect on your experience. For example, which goal did you choose to complete, why did you choose this goal, how did you feel if you completed the goal, and if you didn't manage to complete the goal then what got in the way?

If you haven't already done so then in the next week please try to complete the bold goal from the *work and career* domain. If you have already completed both the small and bold goals from Week 9 (or if it isn't appropriate to complete the bold goal this week), then please use the space below to write a couple more goals for this domain to complete over the next week.

What is Willingness?

Let's start to think about those four ACT processes – willingness, defusion, contact with the present moment and the observing self – that we introduced in Week 8. Perhaps take a look back at them now to refresh your memory – they're on page 43.

We'll begin with willingness. Pursuing as full, rich and meaningful a life as possible while accepting the pain and struggles that inevitably come with it would seem a reasonable trade off. But in everyday life most of us are fine about the first half of that deal and generally less keen about the second half! That is fair enough, as no one wants to experience pain and difficulty.

Yet here's the rub – if we are going to live a rich and fulfilling life, then we cannot avoid the hurt and pain that comes with it. If we want the ups, then we have to be prepared for the downs. If we want to be loved, then we must face the fear of rejection and loss. If we want success, then we must also be ready for failure. We can't have one without the other. This is easy to say and understand, but living it is hard.

In some ways this is the most important message in this diary – life brings both the good and the bad and to live it fully we have to be prepared to embrace both. And that's the deal, whether we like it or not. Rather than trying to get rid of unwanted thoughts and feelings, willingness involves inviting them in, and making a space for them in life (and in the process maybe even discovering that they aren't quite as bad as we initially thought!). This won't sound very appealing on its own, but it opens up the possibility of doing the things that matter, and that is what dignifies our struggles.

Summary goal for the week

Monday 28

Tuesday 1

Wednesday 2

March 2022 Week 10

Thursday

Friday

Saturday

Sunday

*You can't stay in your corner of
the Forest waiting for others to come to you.
You have to go to them sometimes.*

A.A. Milne

Week 11

Welcome to Week 11.

How did you get on? Did you complete the bold goal (or an alternative goal) from the *work and career* domain? Please take a moment to reflect on your experience. For example, which goal did you choose to complete, why did you choose this goal, how did you feel if you completed the goal, and if you didn't manage to complete the goal then what got in the way?

Domain 3: Family Relationships

From the values lists in Week 5 and Week 6, which value would you like to bring to life in the domain of *family relationships*?

Please write a very small commitment, which aligns with this value, and is in this domain, to be completed over the next week.

Now please write a bold commitment, which aligns with this value, and is in this domain, to be completed over the next two weeks.

Please make a note of the barriers (both internal and external) that you think might stop you from completing these goals.

March 2022 Week 11

Summary goal for the week

7 Monday

8 Tuesday

9 Wednesday

March 2022 Week 11

Thursday

Friday

Saturday

Sunday

Life is beautiful. It's about giving. It's about family.

Walt Disney

Week 12

Welcome to Week 12.

How did you get on? Did you complete the small goal from the *family relationships* domain? Please take a moment to reflect on your experience. For example, which goal did you choose to complete, why did you choose this goal, how did you feel if you completed the goal, and if you didn't manage to complete the goal then what got in the way?

If you haven't already done so then in the next week please try to complete the bold goal from the *family relationships* domain. If you have already completed both the small and bold goals from Week 11 (or if it isn't appropriate to complete the bold goal this week), then please use the space below to write a couple more goals for this domain to complete over the next week.

Exploring Willingness – The Unwelcome Guest

Sometimes metaphors can be really effective in helping us understand certain concepts. See if this metaphor helps you to understand willingness. Meet Sam, like a lot of people he wants to have a party with his friends and enjoy himself. Again, like a lot of people, he wants his guests to have a good time and finds himself feeling anxious about this.

Then just when the party is in full flow Joe shows up. Sam doesn't really like Joe and doesn't want him there. And since his arrival, Sam has felt Joe's been ruining the party. Sam asks Joe to leave but he won't go away, so instead Sam ushers Joe into a back room and guards the door. Only now Sam is missing out on the party too. He longs to re-join it but knows that Joe will follow him and that is the last thing he wants to happen.

Joe is an unwelcome guest, like Sam's anxiety. Sam struggles in vain to get rid of or control his anxious thoughts and feelings, but like Joe they just won't leave. Of course, all the time and effort he puts into trying not to feel anxious means he is less engaged with the party. So what can Sam do? Well, one option is to welcome Joe into the party. Sam will still feel annoyed but at least he can be with his friends rather than waste his time trying to control Joe.

March 2022 Week 12

Summary goal for the week

14 Monday

15 Tuesday

16 Wednesday

March 2022 Week 12

Thursday

Friday

Saturday

Sunday

When I let go of what I am,
I become what I might be.

Lao Tzu

Week 13

Welcome to Week 13.

How did you get on? Did you complete the bold goal (or an alternative goal) from the *family relationships* domain? Please take a moment to reflect on your experience. For example, which goal did you choose to complete, why did you choose this goal, how did you feel if you completed the goal, and if you didn't manage to complete the goal then what got in the way?

Domain 4: Education and Learning

From the values lists in Week 5 and Week 6, which value would you like to bring to life in the domain of *education and learning*?

Please write a very small commitment, which aligns with this value, and is in this domain, to be completed over the next week.

Now please write a bold commitment, which aligns with this value, and is in this domain, to be completed over the next two weeks.

Please make a note of the barriers (both internal and external) that you think might stop you from completing these goals.

Summary goal for the week

21 Monday

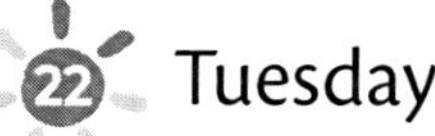

22 Tuesday

23 Wednesday

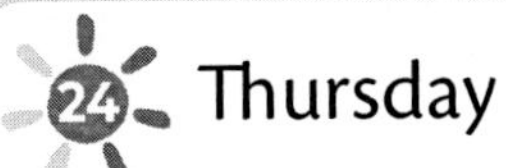

Thursday

Friday

Saturday

Sunday

"Education is not the filling of a pail, but the lighting of a fire."

W.B. Yeats

Week 14

Welcome to Week 14.

How did you get on? Did you complete the small goal from the *education and learning* domain? Please take a moment to reflect on your experience. For example, which goal did you choose to complete, why did you choose this goal, how did you feel if you completed the goal, and if you didn't manage to complete the goal then what got in the way?

If you haven't already done so then in the next week please try to complete the bold goal from the *education and learning* domain. If you have already completed both the small and bold goals from Week 13 (or if it isn't appropriate to complete the bold goal this week), then please use the space below to write a couple more goals for this domain to complete over the next week.

What is Defusion?

The second ACT process that may be useful in helping us to skilfully manage internal barriers is called defusion. One of the challenges we all face is something called fusion (or sometimes *cognitive fusion*). This is when we become tangled up in our thoughts and believe them to be literally true. Fusion can be problematic because when we really believe our thoughts they can have an undue influence on how we behave. They can almost feel like a command to be followed and this can cause difficulties when they are inaccurate, unhelpful or just plain wrong. For example, if we fuse with the thought *'I can't do that'*, then this is likely to stop us even trying.

Defusion involves a very interesting change of focus. Specifically, instead of questioning the truth of our thoughts, all thoughts are instead evaluated on the basis of their usefulness. In other words, we step back and ask ourselves the question: *'Would acting on this thought help me move in a valued life direction?'*

As an example, the thought *'I'm going to become stressed out if I go into that exam hall'* is probably true. However, it isn't very useful if it stops us from going into the exam hall when our education and careers are important to us. Defusion in this context would involve stepping back from the thought and choosing our behaviour carefully based on our values.

March 2022 Week 14

Summary goal for the week

28 Monday

29 Tuesday

30 Wednesday

March/April 2022 Week 14

Thursday

Friday

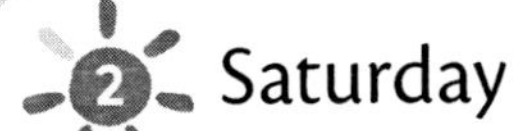

Saturday

Sunday

> *We can't solve problems*
> *by using the same kind of thinking*
> *we used when we created them.*
>
> ***Albert Einstein***

Space for general reflection

Use this space to record the ups and downs of the past few weeks. You may also want to write down what you have learned about yourself and the nature of life.

Week 15

Welcome to Week 15.

How did you get on? Did you complete the bold goal (or an alternative goal) from the *education and learning* domain? Please take a moment to reflect on your experience. For example, which goal did you choose to complete, why did you choose this goal, how did you feel if you completed the goal, and if you didn't manage to complete the goal then what got in the way?

Domain 5: Intimate Relationships

From the values lists in Week 5 and Week 6, which value would you like to bring to life in the domain of *intimate relationships*?

Please write a very small commitment, which aligns with this value, and is in this domain, to be completed over the next week.

Now please write a bold commitment, which aligns with this value, and is in this domain, to be completed over the next two weeks.

Please make a note of the barriers (both internal and external) that you think might stop you from completing these goals.

April 2022 Week 15

Summary goal for the week

4 Monday

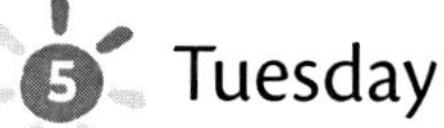

5 Tuesday

6 Wednesday

April 2022 Week 15

Thursday

Friday

Saturday

Sunday

"Love does not consist in gazing at each other, but in looking outward together in the same direction."

Antoine de Sainte-Expury

Week 16

Welcome to Week 16.

How did you get on? Did you complete the small goal from the *intimate relationships* domain? Please take a moment to reflect on your experience. For example, which goal did you choose to complete, why did you choose this goal, how did you feel if you completed the goal, and if you didn't manage to complete the goal then what got in the way?

If you haven't already done so then in the next week please try to complete the bold goal from the *intimate relationships* domain. If you have already completed both the small and bold goals from Week 15 (or if it isn't appropriate to complete the bold goal this week), then please use the space below to write a couple more goals for this domain to complete over the next week.

Exploring Defusion – Having the Thought

Consider this proposition – thoughts, even when they are true, don't have to cause our behaviour. This might sound a little odd at first but try this – think to yourself (or even say out loud) *'Nod your head'*. Repeat this several times and at the same time keep your head still. How did you get on? Did you manage to keep your head still? We bet you did but how is this possible if thoughts control what we do? You can repeat this exercise with any instruction and you will have the same outcome (i.e. thoughts don't have to cause you to behave in certain ways; you can think or say one thing and then act differently).

A great way to reduce the impact that thoughts have on our behaviour is to step back from them by adding the prefix *'I'm having the thought that'* to the thoughts that push us around. This prefix creates a little more space between our thoughts and us, such that we are freer to choose our behaviour.

For example, imagine you had the thought *'I am so bad at first dates that there is no point in ever going on one'*. If you use the prefix it becomes *'I am having the thought that I am so bad at first dates that there is no point in ever going on one'*. Did you notice the shift? In the first instance you probably weren't going to be going on any first dates any time soon, but in the second instance that behaviour felt more likely.

April 2022 — Week 16

Summary goal for the week

11 Monday

12 Tuesday

13 Wednesday

Thursday

Friday

Saturday

Sunday

When in doubt
do the courageous thing.

Jan Smuts

Week 17

Welcome to Week 17.

How did you get on? Did you complete the bold goal (or an alternative goal) from the *intimate relationships* domain? Please take a moment to reflect on your experience. For example, which goal did you choose to complete, why did you choose this goal, how did you feel if you completed the goal, and if you didn't manage to complete the goal then what got in the way?

Domain 6: Self-development and Growth

From the values lists in Week 5 and Week 6, which value would you like to bring to life in the domain of *self-development and growth*?

Please write a very small commitment, which aligns with this value, and is in this domain, to be completed over the next week.

Now please write a bold commitment, which aligns with this value, and is in this domain, to be completed over the next two weeks.

Please make a note of the barriers (both internal and external) that you think might stop you from completing these goals.

April 2022 Week 17

Summary goal for the week

18 Monday

19 Tuesday

20 Wednesday

Thursday

Friday

Saturday

Sunday

> *What really matters is what you do with what you have.*
>
> *H.G. Wells*

Week 18

Welcome to Week 18.

How did you get on? Did you complete the small goal from the *self-development and growth* domain? Please take a moment to reflect on your experience. For example, which goal did you choose to complete, why did you choose this goal, how did you feel if you completed the goal, and if you didn't manage to complete the goal then what got in the way?

If you haven't already done so then in the next week please try to complete the bold goal from the *self-development and growth* domain. If you have already completed both the small and bold goals from Week 17 (or if it isn't appropriate to complete the bold goal this week), then please use the space below to write a couple more goals for this domain to complete over the next week.

What is Contact with the Present Moment?

The third ACT process that can help us to manage thoughts and feelings, and that is often referred to as 'mindfulness' in contemporary culture, is called contact with the present moment. We are so easily dragged into the past or the future that we fail to be in touch with what is going on around us in the present.

Mindfulness involves paying attention to what we are experiencing, on purpose, with an attitude of curiosity. If we are mindful, we notice when our minds have strayed and gently re-orient our attention to what is important in the now.

It sounds simple, and in many ways it is, but it is surprisingly hard to sustain. The reason for this is that the thoughts that go through our minds can pull us away from the present moment and lead us back into the past or forward into the future. However, although mindfulness can be tricky, the good news is that it is a skill, and like all skills, the more we practice it, the better we get.

April 2022 Week 18

Summary goal for the week

25 Monday

26 Tuesday

27 Wednesday

April/May 2022 Week 18

28 Thursday

29 Friday

30 Saturday

1 Sunday

> *Be happy in the moment, that's enough. Each moment is all we need, not more.*
>
> *Mother Teresa*

Space for general reflection

Use this space to record the ups and downs of the past few weeks. You may also want to write down what you have learned about yourself and the nature of life.

Week 19

Welcome to Week 19.

How did you get on? Did you complete the bold goal (or an alternative goal) from the *self-development and growth* domain? Please take a moment to reflect on your experience. For example, which goal did you choose to complete, why did you choose this goal, how did you feel if you completed the goal, and if you didn't manage to complete the goal then what got in the way?

Domain 7: Recreation and Leisure

From the values lists in Week 5 and Week 6, which value would you like to bring to life in the domain of *recreation and leisure*?

Please write a very small commitment, which aligns with this value, and is in this domain, to be completed over the next week.

Now please write a bold commitment, which aligns with this value, and is in this domain, to be completed over the next two weeks.

Please make a note of the barriers (both internal and external) that you think might stop you from completing these goals.

May 2022 Week 19

Summary goal for the week

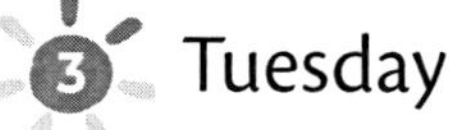

2 Monday

3 Tuesday

4 Wednesday

Thursday

Friday

Saturday

Sunday

The time you enjoy wasting is not wasted time.

Bertrand Russell

Week 20

Welcome to Week 20.

How did you get on? Did you complete the small goal from the *recreation and leisure* domain? Please take a moment to reflect on your experience. For example, which goal did you choose to complete, why did you choose this goal, how did you feel if you completed the goal, and if you didn't manage to complete the goal then what got in the way?

If you haven't already done so then in the next week please try to complete the bold goal from the *recreation and leisure* domain. If you have already completed both the small and bold goals from Week 19 (or if it isn't appropriate to complete the bold goal this week), then please use the space below to write a couple more goals for this domain to complete over the next week.

Exploring Contact with the Present Moment – Breathing

Have you ever tried to train a puppy to sit? If not, let us tell you what happens. Every time you say *'sit'*, the puppy runs off. When this happens we do not get angry or cross with the puppy because they are just doing what puppies do. Our minds are like puppies (they keep running off to different places). Contrary to common assumptions, the point of mindfulness isn't to train our puppy-like mind to sit and stay, it is to simply notice that we have puppy-like minds that will probably be puppy-like forever. Once we begin to notice where our puppy-like minds wander off to (into thoughts or memories), then we will be better able to reorient our attention back to the present moment.

Let's try a mindfulness of breath exercise to introduce you to your puppy-like mind. All you have to do in this task is to breathe in and out ten times. However, as you do this, we want you to try to bring all of your attention to the process of breathing (i.e. only think about your breath). Each time that your mind wanders, notice this has happened and gently reconnect with the experience of your breath, like the rise and fall of your chest or the in and out movement of your stomach.

How did you get on? We'd bet that your mind strayed to many different thoughts about the past and the future, and in doing so, introduced you to your puppy like mind and to the purpose of mindfulness: to re-contact the present moment when our minds have wandered.

May 2022 Week 20

Summary goal for the week

9 Monday

10 Tuesday

11 Wednesday

Thursday

Friday

Saturday

Sunday

Every moment is a golden one for him who has the vision to recognize it as such.

Henry Miller

Week 21

Welcome to Week 21.

How did you get on? Did you complete the bold goal (or an alternative goal) from the *recreation and leisure* domain? Please take a moment to reflect on your experience. For example, which goal did you choose to complete, why did you choose this goal, how did you feel if you completed the goal, and if you didn't manage to complete the goal then what got in the way?

Domain 8: Spirituality

From the values lists in Week 5 and Week 6, which value would you like to bring to life in the domain of *spirituality*? Sometimes, people do not deem spirituality as an important domain. If that is the case for you then please complete this page with more general values and goals in mind.

Please write a very small commitment, which aligns with this value, and is in this domain, to be completed over the next week.

Now please write a bold commitment, which aligns with this value, and is in this domain, to be completed over the next two weeks.

Please make a note of the barriers (both internal and external) that you think might stop you from completing these goals.

May 2022 Week 21

Summary goal for the week

16 Monday

17 Tuesday

18 Wednesday

Thursday

Friday

Saturday

Sunday

"Ordinary riches can be stolen, real riches cannot. In your soul are infinitely precious things that cannot be taken from you."

Oscar Wilde

Week 22

Welcome to Week 22.

How did you get on? Did you complete the small goal from the *spirituality* domain? Please take a moment to reflect on your experience. For example, which goal did you choose to complete, why did you choose this goal, how did you feel if you completed the goal, and if you didn't manage to complete the goal then what got in the way?

If you haven't already done so then in the next week please try to complete the bold goal from the *spirituality* domain. If you have already completed both the small and bold goals from Week 21 (or if it isn't appropriate to complete the bold goal this week), then please use the space below to write a couple more goals for this domain to complete over the next week.

What is the Observing Self?

The last ACT process that can help you to manage tricky thoughts and feelings is called the observing self. In ACT there is an old saying: *'Kill your self every day'*. Of course, this doesn't mean literally to kill yourself; it means that over time we build stories about *'who we are'*, but that often these stories can hold us back. Therefore, kill your stories about *'who you are'* every day so that you can escape their grasp.

When we start to think about who we are in this way, the impossible becomes possible:

- If we kill the self-story that we are not clever enough to go for a promotion, we get to try for that promotion.
- If we kill the self-story that we are not mentally tough enough to lose weight, we get to go to the gym and try.
- If we kill the self-story that we are not a sociable sort of person, we get to try to connect with people.

The observing self, rather than being caught up in our stories, simply watches them. It can be thought of as a container for all of our experiences, the stable and ongoing sense of 'I' that exists independently of the stories that our minds might feed us. When we begin to see ourselves like this then the extent that our stories define us will fall away and we will be more able to choose better ways to behave.

May 2022 Week 22

Summary goal for the week

Monday

Tuesday

25

Wednesday

May 2022 Week 22

Thursday

Friday

Saturday

Sunday

"Self-observation brings man
to the realization of the necessity of self-change."

George Gurdjieff

Space for general reflection

Use this space to record the ups and downs of the past few weeks. You may also want to write down what you have learned about yourself and the nature of life.

Week 23

Welcome to Week 23.

How did you get on? Did you complete the bold goal (or an alternative goal) from the *spirituality* domain? Please take a moment to reflect on your experience. For example, which goal did you choose to complete, why did you choose this goal, how did you feel if you completed the goal, and if you didn't manage to complete the goal then what got in the way?

Domain 9: Community and Citizenship

From the values lists in Week 5 and Week 6, which value would you like to bring to life in the domain of *community and citizenship*?

Please write a very small commitment, which aligns with this value, and is in this domain, to be completed over the next week.

Now please write a bold commitment, which aligns with this value, and is in this domain, to be completed over the next two weeks.

Please make a note of the barriers (both internal and external) that you think might stop you from completing these goals.

May/June 2022 Week 23

Summary goal for the week

30 Monday

Tuesday

Wednesday

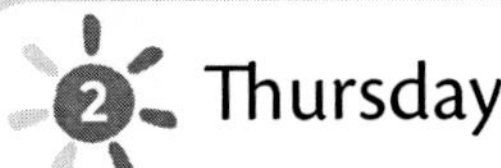

Thursday

Friday

Saturday

Sunday

We must learn to live together as brothers, or perish together as fools.

Martin Luther King, Jr.

Week 24

Welcome to Week 24.

How did you get on? Did you complete the small goal from the *community and citizenship* domain? Please take a moment to reflect on your experience. For example, which goal did you choose to complete, why did you choose this goal, how did you feel if you completed the goal, and if you didn't manage to complete the goal then what got in the way?

If you haven't already done so then in the next week please try to complete the bold goal from the *community and citizenship* domain. If you have already completed both the small and bold goals from Week 23 (or if it isn't appropriate to complete the bold goal this week), then please use the space below to write a couple more goals for this domain to complete over the next week.

Exploring the Observing Self – The Sky and the Weather

A metaphor that nicely illustrates the observing self (which can be a difficult concept to understand) is the relationship between the sky and the weather.

You are like the sky. Your thoughts and feelings are like the weather. The weather changes constantly. Sometimes there is sunshine. However, sometimes there are clouds, wind, rain or storms. Your thoughts and feelings are like this. Sometimes they are happy. However, sometimes they are sad, angry, worried or anxious. There are a couple of important things to know about the relationship between the sky and the weather. Firstly, the weather can never hurt the sky in the same way that your thoughts and feelings can never physically hurt you. Secondly, the sky can always hold the weather no matter how bad it is. You are the same: you can make room for tricky thoughts and feelings no matter how bad they seem.

Sometimes we forget that the sky is there – perhaps it is hard to see the sky through the weather. When this happens it is easy to believe that our thoughts and our self-stories are the sky. They are us. However, every now and then you notice the sky; stable, broad, limitless and pure. The observing self involves learning to access the sky more, and seeing it as a place where we can make room for, and watch, difficult thoughts and feelings about ourselves, rather than be defined by them.

June 2022 Week 24

Summary goal for the week

6 Monday

7 Tuesday

8 Wednesday

June 2022 Week 24

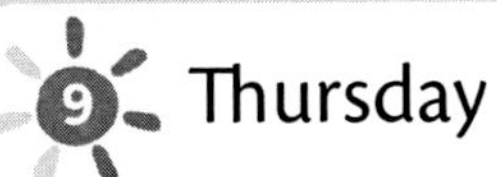

9 Thursday

10 Friday

11 Saturday

12 Sunday

*Do not be angry with the rain;
it simply does not know how to fall upwards.*

Vladimir Nabokov

Week 25

Welcome to Week 25.

How did you get on? Did you complete the bold goal (or an alternative goal) from the *community and citizenship* domain? Please take a moment to reflect on your experience. For example, which goal did you choose to complete, why did you choose this goal, how did you feel if you completed the goal, and if you didn't manage to complete the goal then what got in the way?

Domain 10: Health and Physical Wellbeing

From the values lists in Week 5 and Week 6, which value would you like to bring to life in the domain of *health and physical wellbeing*?

Please write a very small commitment, which aligns with this value, and is in this domain, to be completed over the next week.

Now please write a bold commitment, which aligns with this value, and is in this domain, to be completed over the next two weeks.

Please make a note of the barriers (both internal and external) that you think might stop you from completing these goals.

June 2022 Week 25

Summary goal for the week

13 Monday

Tuesday

15 Wednesday

June 2022

16 Thursday

17 Friday

18 Saturday

19 Sunday

> "Better keep yourself clean and bright. You are the window through which you must see the world."
>
> *George Bernard Shaw*

Week 26

Welcome to Week 26.

How did you get on? Did you complete the small goal from the *health and physical wellbeing* domain? Please take a moment to reflect on your experience. For example, which goal did you choose to complete, why did you choose this goal, how did you feel if you completed the goal, and if you didn't manage to complete the goal then what got in the way?

If you haven't already done so then in the next week please try to complete the bold goal from the *health and physical wellbeing* domain. If you have already completed both the small and bold goals from Week 25 (or if it isn't appropriate to complete the bold goal this week), then please use the space below to write a couple more goals for this domain to complete over the next week.

What is the Hexaflex?

It is exactly half way through the year! We hope that three things are happening for you. Firstly, we hope that bringing a greater focus to values and goals is positively impacting your life. Secondly, we hope you see that values exist independent of the goals you set (i.e. values can trickle into your life as and when the situation calls for it). You may like to make a note when this happens. The third thing we hope is that you are beginning to understand what ACT is all about. In fact, you have now been introduced to the six parts that comprise the ACT model, which is often illustrated using the diagram below. The idea is that you can use any or all of the four processes on the left-hand side of the *hexaflex* to help you more skillfully relate to your thoughts and feelings, such that you are then freer to move towards your values/goals.

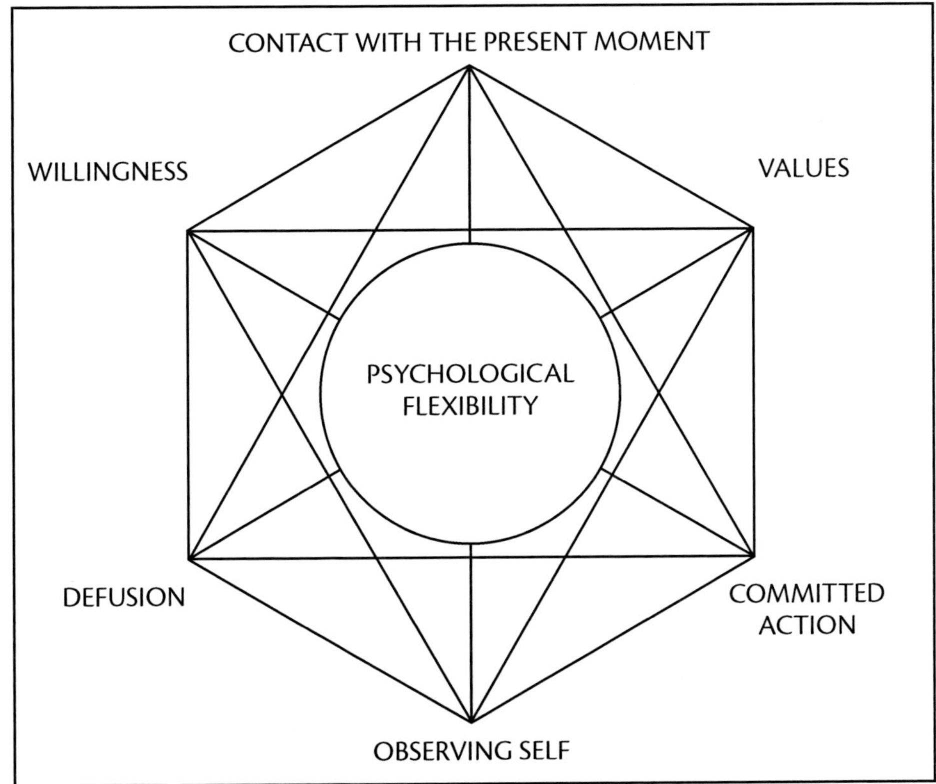

June 2022 Week 26

Summary goal for the week

20 Monday

21 Tuesday

22 Wednesday

June 2022 Week 26

Thursday

Friday

Saturday

Sunday

"Believe you can and you're halfway there."

Theodore Roosevelt

Week 27

Welcome to Week 27.

How did you get on? Did you complete the bold goal (or an alternative goal) from the *health and physical wellbeing* domain? Please take a moment to reflect on your experience. For example, which goal did you choose to complete, why did you choose this goal, how did you feel if you completed the goal, and if you didn't manage to complete the goal then what got in the way?

A Values Exercise – Writing a Eulogy

Now that we've explored values across various domains we're going to ask you to complete a powerful values exercise in the hope that it can clarify your most important values. In fact, you may need the core ACT processes detailed in the hexaflex to help you manage the discomfort that this exercise can provoke (note: keep yourself safe – if you don't fancy this exercise then don't do it).

Imagine for a second that you had died. And that at the funeral, the three most important people in your life stood up and spoke about you. In an absolutely ideal world, what would you like those people to say? Please write this below.

In your answer, you will have detailed the sort of qualities you'd like to embody in this world (or your values). Please choose one and write a value-consistent goal below that you can complete over the next week.

Summary goal for the week

27 Monday

28 Tuesday

29 Wednesday

June/July 2022 Week 27

Thursday

Friday

Saturday

Sunday

> *I don't have any regrets because I'm very optimistic, and live each day as though it's the last.*
>
> ***Michael Caine***

Space for general reflection

Use this space to record the ups and downs of the past few weeks. You may also want to write down what you have learned about yourself and the nature of life.

Week 28

Welcome to Week 28.

How did you get on? Did you complete the goal from the eulogy exercise? Please take a moment to reflect on your experience. For example, what was the goal, why did you choose it, how did you feel if you completed it, and if you didn't complete it then what got in the way?

Please now return to your answer from the eulogy exercise in Week 27 and record another values-consistent goal below, to complete in the next week.

Introducing Self-Compassion

The thing about setting goals, both in the context of this diary and in the context of our lives more broadly, is that often we fail to complete them! We are going to assume that this has happened many times already this year for you. When we do fail to meet our goals we human beings tend to pick up a big stick and hit ourselves with it, metaphorically speaking. Not only that, but while we are busy beating ourselves up we somehow manage to give up on our goals, as if they are lost forever. For many of us this is all too familiar, but is there a better way, you could even say a more useful way, to respond to ourselves when we mess up? How about a bit of self-compassion?

Compassion is comprised of two distinct parts – it's about being sensitive to other people's distress *and* being motivated to do something about it. When we have compassion, we feel another's pain and make efforts to support them with it. Self-compassion is essentially the same process; only it involves acting in this way towards ourselves. It involves noticing our critical minds, our pain or aspects of ourselves that we don't like and responding with kindness, patience and understanding.

In other words, instead of ignoring our suffering or just relentlessly criticising ourselves for our inadequacies, we try to ask the following question when we have failed *'What can I do to care for myself, or be kind to myself, right now?'*

July 2022 Week 28

Summary goal for the week

4 Monday

5 Tuesday

6 Wednesday

If your compassion does not include yourself, it's incomplete.

The Buddha

Week 29

Welcome to Week 29.

How did you get on? Did you complete another goal from the eulogy exercise? Please take a moment to reflect on your experience. For example, what was the goal, why did you choose it, how did you feel if you completed it, and if you didn't complete it then what got in the way?

For the final time, please now return to your answer from the eulogy exercise in Week 27 and record another values-consistent goal below, to complete in the next week.

Exploring Self-Compassion – Helping a Child

Interestingly, it seems easier to be compassionate than to be self-compassionate. What we are wondering therefore, is whether it is possible to extend the same kindness and support to yourself that you would give so easily to someone you love? This exercise aims to explore that question.

Imagine that you're a teacher in a primary school. One rainy Tuesday morning it's your turn to do playground duty. As you walk around the playground, you notice that one particular little boy is running around too vigorously given the wet conditions. As you make your way over to speak to him, the boy falls really hard on the ground, grazing his knees, hands and nose. He cries and cries.

How would you react? What would you do? Really try to picture it. You might cuddle the little boy. You might tell him that everything is going to be ok. You might make a joke to cheer him up. You might miss your own lunch to sit with him while the nurse begins treatment.

It is amazing how compassionate we can be to other people, but what if that little boy is a metaphor for you in this world? What if you are picking up grazes (failures and mistakes) as you try to manage the trickiness of life? Can you treat yourself with the same kindness that you would so easily give to this little boy?

Summary goal for the week

11 Monday

12 Tuesday

13 Wednesday

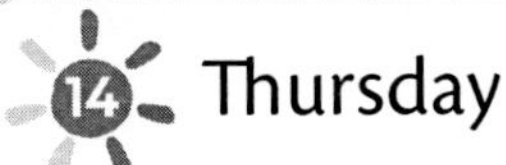

14 Thursday

15 Friday

16 Saturday

17 Sunday

I have always depended on the kindness of strangers.

Tennessee Williams

Week 30

Welcome to Week 30.

How did you get on? Did you complete a third and final goal from the eulogy exercise? Please take a moment to reflect on your experience. For example, what was the goal, why did you choose it, how did you feel if you completed it, and if you didn't complete it then what got in the way?

In the next few weeks, we'd like you to add another layer to your experience of values by writing personal values statements across four broad areas of your life. In between writing these statements we'll introduce you to the notion of experiential avoidance, which forms an important part of the ACT rationale.

Personal Values Statement: Health

Is your *health* important to you? If so, why? Possibly because being healthy will allow you to travel, will allow you to do sport or will allow you to spend time with the people that you love? Have a think about which values might be useful to you in this area, and write a values statement below. An example of a values statement might be *'My health is important to me because it will allow me to play sport as I grow older. Consequently, I would like to be patient and persistent as I attempt to become fitter'*.

Personal Values Statement:

Now, in the spaces below, please record 6 goals that you can complete, short-term and long-term, which would bring you closer to your personal values statement in the area of *health*. Try to complete one or more of these goals in the next week.

1

2

3

4

5

6

July 2022 Week 30

Summary goal for the week

18 Monday

19 Tuesday

20 Wednesday

Thursday

Friday

Saturday

Sunday

Your body is the harp of your soul and it is yours to bring forth sweet music from it.

Kahlil Gibran

Week 31

Welcome to Week 31.

How did you get on? Did you complete any goals related to your personal values statement in the area of *health*? Please take a moment to reflect on your experience. For example, how did you feel if you completed any of the goals, and if you didn't complete some of them then what got in the way?

Please now return to Week 30 (where you wrote a personal values statement in the area of *health*), pick one or more further goals to complete in the next week and write them in the space below.

Introducing Experiential Avoidance

Here is a truth that is not often told – life is tough. No doubt there are times when things are great and we feel content and happy, but often this is not the case. Worries, stresses, fears, regrets, aches and pains all too frequently hold our attention. The carving up of human suffering into conditions can give the impression that these problems are individually rare. However, when we group them together we see that it is quite the opposite – suffering is commonplace. Indeed, it is quite normal.

The problem is human language. Give an animal food, water and social contact in a safe and comfortable place and they will be content. But this is not so for human beings. Even when surrounded by abundance, thanks to our language we can feel scared, sad, concerned or confused at any time by just thinking about certain things. Right now, in this moment, you could bring sorrow into your life by simply recalling a painful memory or imagining an unwanted future.

It would be great if we could turn off our thinking from time-to-time so we could avoid the suffering it can bring. However, experiential avoidance, the attempted removal of unwanted thoughts and feelings from our minds, not only doesn't work but often leads to more problems, as we will explore in the next few weeks.

July 2022 Week 31

Summary goal for the week

25 Monday

26 Tuesday

27 Wednesday

July 2022 Week 31

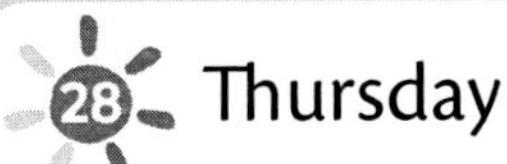

Thursday

Friday

Saturday

Sunday

“I try to avoid looking forward or backward, and try to keep looking upward.”

Charlotte Brontë

Space for general reflection

Use this space to record the ups and downs of the past few weeks. You may also want to write down what you have learned about yourself and the nature of life.

Week 32

Welcome to Week 32.

How did you get on? Did you complete another goal from the personal values statement in the area of *health*? Please take a moment to reflect on your experience. For example, how did you feel if you completed any of the goals, and if you didn't complete some of them then what got in the way?

August 2022

Personal Values Statement: Work

Is your *work* important to you? If so, why? Possibly because it brings you fulfilment or because it allows you to provide for your family? Have a think about which values might be useful to you in this area, and write a values statement below. An example of a values statement might be *'My work is important to me because it allows me to contribute to the lives of others. Consequently, I would like to be creative and enthusiastic as I move forward with my career'*.

Personal Values Statement:

Now, in the spaces below, please record 6 goals that you can complete, short-term and long-term, which would bring you closer to your personal values statement in the area of *work*. Try to complete one or more of these goals in the next week.

1

2

3

4

5

6

August 2022 Week 32

Summary goal for the week

1 Monday

2 Tuesday

3 Wednesday

August 2022 Week 32

Thursday

Friday

Saturday

Sunday

"The only way to do great work is to love what you do. If you haven't found it yet, keep looking."

Steve Jobs

Week 33

Welcome to Week 33.

How did you get on? Did you complete a goal related to your personal values statement in the area of *work*? Please take a moment to reflect on your experience. For example, how did you feel if you completed any of the goals, and if you didn't complete some of them then what got in the way?

Please now return to Week 32 (where you wrote a personal values statement in the area of *work*), pick one or more further goals to complete in the next week and write them in the space below.

Exploring Experiential Avoidance – The White Bear

What would you do if you felt cold, were caught in the rain, or had a stone in your shoe? Most probably you would act in ways that reduced the discomfort you were experiencing. You might, for example, put on a jumper, put up an umbrella, remove the stone or even hop on one leg. Your actions would depend on your particular circumstances but in general they would all have the same aim – to reduce, stop or avoid the discomfort. Avoiding or reducing negative, painful or unpleasant experiences can be a good survival strategy, as it lessens our exposure to events that might harm us. It's easy to see why acting to avoid negative events makes sense and is hard-wired into us by our evolutionary past.

However, a problem emerges when we apply this same strategy to the world inside our skin because we just don't have the same level of control over our internal world as we do over events in the external world. To illustrate how little control we sometimes have over our minds, please complete this popular exercise: *for one minute, try your best to not think about a white bear, if you do think about it then leave a mark on a piece of paper.*

How did you get on? Most people report seeing the dreaded bear on many occasions and in doing so learn that trying our best to avoid certain thoughts may be a futile activity.

Summary goal for the week

8 Monday

9 Tuesday

10 Wednesday

Thursday

Friday

Saturday

Sunday

Fear is a reaction.
Courage is a decision.

Winston Churchill

Week 34

Welcome to Week 34.

How did you get on? Did you complete another goal from the personal values statement in the area of *work*? Please take a moment to reflect on your experience. For example, how did you feel if you completed any of the goals, and if you didn't complete some of them then what got in the way?

Personal Values Statement: Leisure

Is *leisure* important to you? If so, why? Possibly because it helps you to have fun or because it allows you to spend time with friends? Have a think about which values might be useful to you in this area, and write a values statement below. An example of a values statement might be *'My leisure is important to me because it allows me to appreciate spending time with my friends. Consequently, I would like to make time for leisure, and bring humour and challenge to my leisure activities'.*

Personal Values Statement:

Now, in the spaces below, please record 6 goals that you can complete, short-term and long-term, which would bring you closer to your personal values statement in the area of *leisure*. Try to complete one or more of these goals in the next week.

1

2

3

4

5

6

August 2022 Week 34

Summary goal for the week

15 Monday

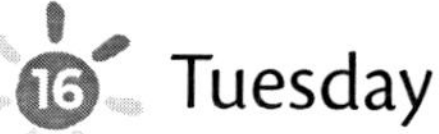

16 Tuesday

17 Wednesday

August 2022 Week 34

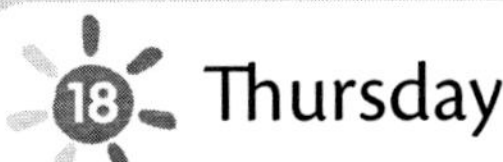

Thursday

Friday

Saturday

Sunday

There is still plenty out there to get motivated by.

Andre Agassi

Week 35

Welcome to Week 35.

How did you get on? Did you complete a goal related to your personal values statement in the area of *leisure*? Please take a moment to reflect on your experience. For example, how did you feel if you completed any of the goals, and if you didn't complete some of them then what got in the way?

Please now return to Week 34 (where you wrote a personal values statement in the area of *leisure*), pick one or more further goals to complete in the next week and write them in the space below.

Exploring Experiential Avoidance – A Crucial Side Effect

In addition to being a futile activity in and of itself, a crucial side effect of avoidance is that it tends to impact our behaviour in negative ways. Specifically, efforts to avoid unwanted thoughts and feelings can lead to avoiding the situations that give rise to them. While this can seem like it solves the initial problem – avoidance of the unwanted thoughts or feelings – we are restricting our lives in the process, which can have a major impact on our wider sense of fulfilment.

For example, if meeting other people makes us anxious, then we could avoid places where they might be. Sounds like a good solution but it also means that our lives become smaller, maybe even limited just to our home. Whilst this might sound extreme, there are thousands of people for whom this is a daily reality. They might not be fully aware of it, but the solution to their first problem has created a second, bigger problem.

When avoidance of discomfort is our primary aim then the amount of value-consistent activities that we can engage in will grow smaller and smaller. This is because sometimes the things that are most important to us are also the things that bring us pain or discomfort.

August 2022 Week 35

Summary goal for the week

22 Monday

Tuesday

24 Wednesday

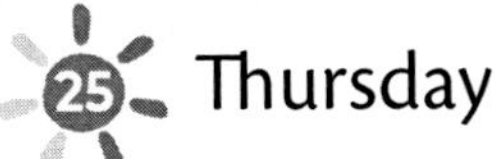

Thursday

Friday

Saturday

Sunday

Whatever it is you're scared of doing, do it.

Neil Gaiman

Week 36

Welcome to Week 36.

How did you get on? Did you complete another goal from the personal values statement in the area of *leisure*? Please take a moment to reflect on your experience. For example, how did you feel if you completed any of the goals, and if you didn't complete some of them then what got in the way?

Personal Values Statement: Relationships

Are *relationships* important to you? If so, why? Possibly because the feeling of human connection brings you meaning or perhaps having healthy relationships allow you to complete other goals? Have a think about which values might be useful to you in this area, and write a values statement below. An example of a values statement might be *'My relationships are important to me because of the energy and love that they bring me. Consequently, I would like to bring kindness, patience and positivity to the people in my life'*.

Personal Values Statement:

Now, in the spaces below, please record 6 goals that you can complete, short-term and long-term, which would bring you closer to your personal values statement in the area of *relationships*. Try to complete one or more of these goals in the next week.

1

2

3

4

5

6

August 2022

Week 36

Summary goal for the week

29 Monday

30 Tuesday

31 Wednesday

September 2022 Week 36

Thursday

Friday

Saturday

Sunday

"When we feel love and kindness toward others, it helps us also to develop inner happiness and peace."

The Dalai Lama

Space for general reflection

Use this space to record the ups and downs of the past few weeks. You may also want to write down what you have learned about yourself and the nature of life.

Week 37

Welcome to Week 37.

How did you get on? Did you complete a goal related to your personal values statement in the area of *relationships*? Please take a moment to reflect on your experience. For example, how did you feel if you completed any of the goals, and if you didn't complete some of them then what got in the way?

Please now return to Week 36 (where you wrote a personal values statement in the area of *relationships*), pick one or more further goals to complete in the next week and write them in the space below.

Exploring Experiential Avoidance – A Ball in the Water

A perfect metaphor for illustrating the impact of engaging in experiential avoidance involves trying to keep a ball submerged underwater.

Imagine that a ball represents your negative thoughts and feelings. You really don't want to have these thoughts and feelings so you try to get rid of them by holding them under the water. As you hold the ball under the water you notice three things. Firstly, that even with your best efforts the ball continues to pop out of the water. Unwanted thoughts and feelings are like this; they are very difficult to suppress. Secondly, you notice that your arms are hurting from trying to hold the ball under the water. Attempted suppression takes a lot of effort. Thirdly, you realise that by fighting with the ball you are missing out on playing games with your friends. Attempted suppression can spill over into valued activities.

To summarise experiential avoidance – while wanting to avoid painful and/or discomforting internal experiences is quite natural, doing so often has negative consequences (i.e. it doesn't work, it takes a lot of effort and it can stop you from engaging in valued activities). It is for this reason that ACT is an approach that involves doing the exact opposite of avoidance.

September 2022 Week 37

Summary goal for the week

5 Monday

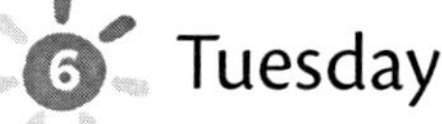

6 Tuesday

7 Wednesday

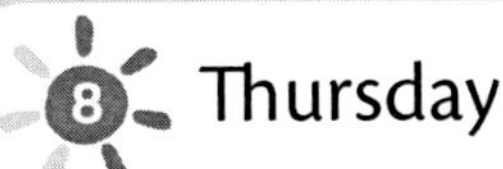

8 Thursday

9 Friday

10 Saturday

11 Sunday

> *I believe every human has a finite number of heartbeats. I don't intend to waste any of mine.*
>
> ***Neil Armstrong***

Week 38

Welcome to Week 38.

How did you get on? Did you complete another goal from the personal values statement in the area of *relationships*? Please take a moment to reflect on your experience. For example, how did you feel if you completed any of the goals, and if you didn't complete some of them then what got in the way?

September 2022

Giving You The Reins

Throughout this diary we have gradually asked you to delve deeper and deeper into your values. At this moment, therefore, you should have a fairly good idea of which domains in your life are most important, and what qualities you would like to turn into action on this earth.

From this point forward, in addition to describing some helpful ACT metaphors across each domain of the hexaflex, we are going to be less prescriptive about how you bring your values to life. Instead, we are going go full circle by asking you again the very first question that you saw in this diary.

What do you want to achieve in the next few months? In the space below please record some values and goals that are important to you at this point in your life, and detail how you might move towards one or more of those goals in the next week.

September 2022 Week 38

Summary goal for the week

12 Monday

13 Tuesday

14 Wednesday

September 2022 Week 38

Thursday

Friday

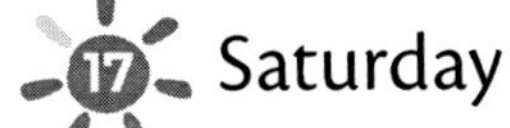

Saturday

Sunday

There is only one thing that makes a dream impossible to achieve: the fear of failure.

Paulo Coelho

Week 39

Welcome to Week 39.

How did you get on? Did you make progress? Take a moment to reflect on your experience. Were your behaviours this week generally value consistent or value inconsistent?

Record some values and goals that are important to you and which you can try to complete in the next week.

Exploring Willingness – Quicksand

The thing about avoidance is that it comes so naturally to us. For example, if there is danger in the outside world then avoidance is a good problem solving strategy. However, that same strategy, when applied to the internal world of our thoughts and feelings, doesn't work. But what might? Well, it is easy enough for us to yell the word *'willingness'* at you right now, but there is no doubt that willingness can feel like an odd thing to do at first, as the quicksand metaphor aims to illustrate.

If you are ever stuck in quicksand then every bone in your body will urge you to keep moving your arms and your legs in an attempt to get out. In other words, your instinct will tell you to struggle with the quicksand. However, the problem with struggling in quicksand is that the more you struggle and fight to get out the more quickly you will get sucked in. In fact, the only way to escape from quicksand, as unnatural as it may feel, is to stop struggling. What you are supposed to do is lie back, spread out your body and be as still as possible.

Willingness to experience unwanted thoughts and feelings is a little bit like this. Our every instinct tells us to get rid of them. However, struggling with our unwanted thoughts and feelings won't work in the same way that struggling with quicksand won't work. Your better option, even though it may feel unnatural, is to take them with you.

September 2022 Week 39

Summary goal for the week

19 Monday

20 Tuesday

21 Wednesday

September 2022 Week 39

Thursday

Friday

Saturday

Sunday

If you were born with the weakness to fall, you were born with the strength to rise.

Rupi Kaur

Week 40

Welcome to Week 40.

How did you get on? Did you make progress? Take a moment to reflect on your experience. Were your behaviours this week generally value consistent or value inconsistent?

Record some values and goals that are important to you and which you can try to complete in the next week.

Exploring Willingness Further – Tug-of-War with a Monster

Do you know what a tug-of-war contest is? Team A holds one end of a rope, Team B holds the other end and between the two teams there is a large puddle of dirty water. One metaphor about a tug-of-war contest can be useful in helping us to think about willingness.

Imagine you are in a tug-of-war contest with a big, ugly monster. Between the two of you is a large and seemingly bottomless hole. If you lose the contest you will surely die. So you start pulling. You look up to see the monster holding the rope with just one hand despite the fact that you are pulling as hard as you can. The monster then decides to take the contest a bit more seriously. He begins pulling and you find yourself moving closer and closer to the hole of death. You pull harder, but he is stronger, so what can you do?

ACT teaches us that we don't need to change our thoughts and feelings. We can instead develop the willingness to experience them. We can acknowledge their existence and get on with the act of living. In other words, ACT helps us to see that we no longer have to win a tug-of-war contest with our monsters; we can learn to drop the rope.

September 2022 Week 40

Summary goal for the week

26 Monday

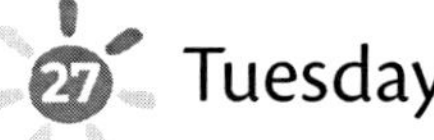

27 Tuesday

28 Wednesday

September/October 2022 Week 40

Thursday

Friday

Saturday

Sunday

> Once we believe in ourselves, we can risk curiosity, wonder, spontaneous delight, or any experience that reveals the human spirit.
>
> *E.E. Cummings*

Space for general reflection

Use this space to record the ups and downs of the past few weeks. You may also want to write down what you have learned about yourself and the nature of life.

Week 41

Welcome to Week 41.

How did you get on? Did you make progress? Take a moment to reflect on your experience. Were your behaviours this week generally value consistent or value inconsistent?

Record some values and goals that are important to you and which you can try to complete in the next week.

Exploring Defusion – Leaves on a Stream

Defusion is all about getting better at watching and noticing our thoughts. A great way to improve defusion skills is via a meditation type exercise that requires you to watch your thoughts like you would watch leaves on a stream. Below are some instructions for how to do this:

1. Close your eyes and picture yourself being sat next to a stream on a warm summers day.
2. Now, for 3 minutes, watch any thoughts that pop into your mind.
3. As you notice a thought, pick it up and place it gently on a leaf that is making its way down the stream.
4. The leaf may hang around for a little bit. That's fine. Don't force its movement. If it hangs around then continue to watch it, if it floats away then watch it float away. Your only job is to notice it.
5. Do this with every thought that you notice, positive and negative.
6. If your mind seems to stop giving you thoughts then wait a while and they will come back. When they do, place them on a leaf.
7. If your mind says *'I'm rubbish at this'* or *'This is a silly exercise'* then place those thoughts on a leaf too.
8. Don't slow down or speed up the leaves. Your job here is only to notice.
9. You will get pulled out of the exercise, at times. When that happens, simply place the next thought on a leaf and continue.

October 2022 Week 41

Summary goal for the week

3 Monday

4 Tuesday

5 Wednesday

October 2022 Week 41

Thursday

Friday

Saturday

Sunday

As soon as you honor the present moment, all unhappiness and struggle dissolve, and life begins to flow with joy and ease.

Eckhart Tolle

Week 42

Welcome to Week 42.

How did you get on? Did you make progress? Take a moment to reflect on your experience. Were your behaviours this week generally value consistent or value inconsistent?

Record some values and goals that are important to you and which you can try to complete in the next week.

Exploring Defusion Further – Hands as Thoughts

In addition to watching our thoughts, a key part of defusion is experiencing how being wrapped up in them can negatively impact our daily life. The *'Hands as Thoughts'* metaphor illustrates this idea.

Bring your hands up to your face and fix them in front of your eyes. What happens to your view of the room when you do this? Is it difficult to concentrate on a particular task? Would you be able to use your hands for anything else whilst they are fixed in front of your face like this? Your thoughts can be like this. When they are very close to us, right up in front of our eyes, they can have a negative impact on us. Specifically, when certain thoughts dominate our existence it can be difficult to notice things going on around us, it can be difficult to concentrate on a particular task, and it can be difficult to take effective action.

Now put your hands in your lap. The thoughts are still there, but you now have a bit of distance from them. As a result you are in a better position to interact with the things going on around you, you are in a better position to concentrate on the tasks in front of you and you are in a better position to act in an effective way.

October 2022 Week 42

Summary goal for the week

10 Monday

11 Tuesday

12 Wednesday

October 2022 Week 42

Thursday

Friday

Saturday

Sunday

It's not what you look at that matters, it's what you see.

Henry David Thoreau

Week 43

Welcome to Week 43.

How did you get on? Did you make progress? Take a moment to reflect on your experience. Were your behaviours this week generally value consistent or value inconsistent?

Record some values and goals that are important to you and which you can try to complete in the next week.

Exploring Mindfulness – The Body Scan

Mindfulness isn't about your ability to focus on your breath per se. Instead, formal mindfulness exercises are used to train a key skill – the ability to bring your attention back to the present moment when your mind has wandered – so that you can use that skill in situations that call for it. Like mindfulness of breath, the body scan is another popular formal mindfulness exercise, which involves bringing attention to different parts of your body. We'd like you to have a go now. Please follow these steps:

- Sit down on a chair and keep your back upright.
- Close your eyes.
- Slowly move your attention to any sensations you might feel in the following parts of your body:

Toes	Ankles	Calves	Hamstrings
Buttocks	Back	Tummy	Chest
Shoulders	Neck	Head	Hands

- As you notice sensations throughout your body, try to notice when your mind has wandered to another topic. When this happens gently re-orient your attention back to the different parts of your body.

Summary goal for the week

17 Monday

18 Tuesday

19 Wednesday

October 2022 Week 43

Thursday

Friday

Saturday

Sunday

Many people are alive but don't touch the miracle of being alive.

Thích Nhất Hạnh

Week 44

Welcome to Week 44.

How did you get on? Did you make progress? Take a moment to reflect on your experience. Were your behaviours this week generally value consistent or value inconsistent?

Record some values and goals that are important to you and which you can try to complete in the next week.

Exploring Mindfulness Further – Walking Aware

As we mentioned in Week 43, mindfulness exercises are about developing skills that can be generalised to other times and situations when you really need them. One way to encourage generalisation is to practice mindfulness as part of your everyday routine. An interesting way to do this is via a mindful walking exercise, which is something we'd like you to do now. If you are willing then please go for a 5-minute walk. Your only job while you walk is to:

1. Notice the things around you.
2. Notice when your mind has wandered away from the things directly in front of you and bring it back to the present moment.

Walking is an activity that we generally do on automatic pilot. Consequently, as it is so easy for our minds to wander when we walk, we often fail to notice the beauty around us. In fact, when walking mindfully, some people report seeing things for the first time, despite the fact that they had walked the route in question on many occasions! This goes to show that not only is it possible to incorporate mindfulness into our daily routine, but that by doing so we will increase our awareness.

Summary goal for the week

24 Monday

25 Tuesday

26 Wednesday

October 2022 Week 44

Thursday

Friday

28

Saturday

29

Sunday

30

> *You don't learn to walk by following rules. You learn by doing, and by falling over.*
>
> ***Richard Branson***

Space for general reflection

Use this space to record the ups and downs of the past few weeks. You may also want to write down what you have learned about yourself and the nature of life.

Week 45

Welcome to Week 45.

How did you get on? Did you make progress? Take a moment to reflect on your experience. Were your behaviours this week generally value consistent or value inconsistent?

Record some values and goals that are important to you and which you can try to complete in the next week.

Exploring the Observing Self – Description and Evaluation

As described in Week 22, we humans so easily build stories about who we think we *'truly'* are and this can be problematic when our stories inhibit what we do. Sometimes a good way of dismantling that way of thinking is to notice the difference between description and evaluation.

For example, suppose I am holding a mobile phone, and I describe it in the following way: *My phone has a black screen, is slightly smaller than my hand and has a camera facility*. Upon seeing my mobile phone you would be able to agree with that sentence from an objective position.

But imagine that I then add the following words to the description: *My phone is the best phone in the world*. At this point you might step in with an objection on the basis that the second sentence isn't a description, it is an evaluation.

We often treat our evaluations as descriptions, which can be unhelpful. For example, we might think of ourselves as not being smart, which is actually closer to an evaluation than a description. In the space below, please complete the *'I am'* sentences with information about you, then circle the statements that are probably evaluation and not fact, because those statements are the ones to watch out for.

I am	I am
I am	I am
I am	I am
I am	I am
I am	I am

Summary goal for the week

31 Monday

1 Tuesday

2 Wednesday

November 2022 Week 45

Thursday

Friday

Saturday

Sunday

*Don't be satisfied with stories,
how things have gone with others.
Unfold your own myth.*

Rumi

Week 46

Welcome to Week 46.

How did you get on? Did you make progress? Take a moment to reflect on your experience. Were your behaviours this week generally value consistent or value inconsistent?

Record some values and goals that are important to you and which you can try to complete in the next week.

Exploring the Observing Self Further – Who is Noticing?

A good way for you to access your observing self, the stable sense of 'I' that exists independently of your thoughts, feelings and stories about yourself, is to engage in a brief mindfulness exercise that requires you to notice who is doing the noticing.

Begin by closing your eyes. Then, for 30 seconds, simply listen to what your mind has to say. The thoughts may be positive or negative, they may be descriptive or evaluative, and they may even stop for a while. Your job for this 30-second period is simply to watch what happens.

What did you notice? Most people will report mind wandering, as they might do in any typical mindfulness exercise. However, we want you to notice something else. Specifically, we want you to notice that the exercise involved two selves. One 'self', let's call it your *thinking self*, provided you with your thoughts and feelings. Sometimes, it can seem as though we only have a thinking self. But who was watching and listening to the chatter of the thinking self? Who was observing? This is your second sense of self. That is, your *observing self* was there too. Listening, noticing, observing.

November 2022 Week 46

Summary goal for the week

7 Monday

8 Tuesday

9 Wednesday

Thursday

Friday

12 Saturday

Sunday

Find out who you are and do it on purpose.

Dolly Parton

Week 47

Welcome to Week 47.

How did you get on? Did you make progress? Take a moment to reflect on your experience. Were your behaviours this week generally value consistent or value inconsistent?

Exploring Values – Your Heroes

Now that we have further explored the left hand side of the hexaflex, let's look for a final time at your values. One exercise that may be useful at this point involves describing your heroes. In the space below, please name three of your heroes, and detail why they are your heroes.

Some values will pop out of your answers above. That is, some of the qualities that you see in your heroes are probably qualities that you would like to see in yourself. Choose one such value and in the space below record a goal for the coming week that is in line with it.

November 2022 Week 47

Summary goal for the week

14 Monday

15 Tuesday

16 Wednesday

Thursday

Friday

Saturday

Sunday

Everybody is a hero in their own story if you just look.

Maeve Binchy

Week 48

Welcome to Week 48.

How did you get on? Did you complete the goal related to the heroes exercise? Please take a moment to reflect on your experience. For example, what did you think and/or feel before, during and after you had completed your goal? Also, were your behaviours this week generally value consistent or value inconsistent? Perhaps list notable behaviours in both of those categories?

Please now choose another value from the heroes exercise and in the space below record a bold goal that is in line with it to be completed over the next week.

Exploring Committed Action – Waiting for the Wrong Train

The one part of the hexaflex that we haven't yet spoken about explicitly in this diary is committed action. The reason for this is because we have actually asked you to engage in committed action every week by asking you to complete goals. However, now may be the time to think a little bit about it. Why? Because although committed action sounds simple, as you try to act in value consistent ways many unwanted thoughts and feelings may appear. When they do, you will want to continue with your plans for committed action, as the following metaphor illustrates.

Imagine that you are going on a journey to a place that is very special to you (your values). When you get to the train station (the point at which action is required) you see two trains, both of which make the promise of going to your destination. The first train is dirty and uncomfortable. As the second train looks safe and reliable, you decide that it is the better way to travel. However, as you sit on the comfortable train you notice that it never moves. The dirty and uncomfortable train makes many journeys, but your train just doesn't move. Soon you realise that the safe train may never move, and that, in fact, you are sat on the wrong train.

When you attempt to move forward, your mind will try to keep you safe. However, sometimes safety can be akin to being stuck. Sometimes, journeys to a special place may be uncomfortable, but that is not a reason to not make the journey.

November 2022 Week 48

Summary goal for the week

21 Monday

Tuesday

23 Wednesday

November 2022 Week 48

Thursday

Friday

Saturday

Sunday

Don't be afraid to expand yourself, to step out of your comfort zone. That's where the joy and adventure lie.

Herbie Hancock

Week 49

Welcome to Week 49.

How did you get on with completing a second goal from the heroes exercise? Please take a moment to reflect on your experience. For example, what did you think and/or feel before, during and after you had completed your goal? Also, were your behaviours this week generally value consistent or value inconsistent? Perhaps list notable behaviours in both of those categories?

In these last few weeks we'd like you to choose some values and goals that seem most important right now. What are the most important changes you'd like to make? Please write a goal or two in the space below to complete in the next week.

Bringing it all Together: Driving the Bus

Sometimes our minds are just not good for us. They can come up with endless reasons to do or not do different things, and if we pay too much attention to what they say then this can stop us getting on with what we really want to do. Imagine you are about to go to the gym or call a friend, how often has your mind interjected with *'I'm too tired'* or *'I'll do it tomorrow instead'*? It's not that minds are bad or faulty; it's just that they are quick to come up with reasons for not doing things, even when those things matter to us. Starting now (and continuing over the next few weeks), we will describe a popular ACT metaphor that may help you understand the way in which our minds work, and how we often listen to them when we shouldn't.

Imagine that you are a bus driver. You get to drive your bus wherever you like. This is much like your life; you get to move in directions (i.e. values) that are important to you. So here you are, driving your bus of life, and in the distance you see somewhere that you want to go, a place that you would love to get to. For argument's sake, let's call it *lose weight*. Imagine that you start driving towards this place (you are about to go for a run). In the space below please write down some unhelpful thoughts that might pop into your mind.

November 2022 Week 49

Summary goal for the week

28 Monday

29 Tuesday

30 Wednesday

December 2022 Week 49

Thursday

Friday

Saturday

Sunday

> *The important work of moving the world forward does not wait to be done by perfect men.*
>
> ***George Eliot***

Space for general reflection

Use this space to record the ups and downs of the past few weeks. You may also want to write down what you have learned about yourself and the nature of life.

Week 50

Welcome to Week 50.

How did you get on with your goals? Did you make progress? Take a moment to reflect on your experience. Were your behaviours this week generally value consistent or value inconsistent?

In the space below please record some values and goals that are important to you at this point in your life. Try to complete one or more of them in the next week.

Bringing it all Together: Passenger Revolt!

So you start driving towards this place that you want to get to and as you do a number of passengers (thoughts) run to the front of the bus and start shouting at you. They can be scary, aggressive, persuasive, sneaky, and are generally unhelpful. They try any way they can to make you drive an alternative route. For example, one passenger might say *'It is too cold to go running now'*.

Imagine that you listened to your passengers and changed your route. What do you think you might feel in the short and the long-term? Please write your thoughts below.

December 2022 Week 50

Summary goal for the week

5 Monday

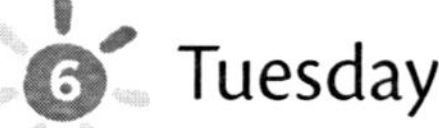

6 Tuesday

7 Wednesday

December 2022 Week 50

8 Thursday

9 Friday

10 Saturday

11 Sunday

> *Courage is about doing what you're afraid to do. There can be no courage unless you're scared.*
>
> **Eddie Rickenbacker**

Week 51

Welcome to Week 51.

How did you get on with your goals? Did you make progress? Take a moment to reflect on your experience. Were your behaviours this week generally value consistent or value inconsistent?

December 2022

Bringing it all Together: Keep on Driving

So you have listened to your passengers and therefore you are not moving in the direction of what is important to you. A few months go by of driving around when you see the goal again. You start driving towards it. The passengers run to the front of the bus and start being unhelpful. However, this time you keep driving. By doing so, you learn three things:

1. Every time you drive towards that special place the passengers show up. Whenever we start moving towards things that are important to us the mind will probably have something unhelpful to say about it.
2. There is no way to remove the passengers or to make them stop in their sneaky ways. Unwanted thoughts and feelings are like this.
3. Most importantly, as persuasive as these passengers are, they don't have to impact OUR behaviour.

In the space below write down a place that you would like to get to (a goal to complete in the next week), and write down the passengers that you think might be on your bus. What might they look like? Which do you think might be the most powerful in altering your behaviour?

?

?

?

Summary goal for the week

12 Monday

13 Tuesday

14 Wednesday

December 2022 Week 51

15 Thursday

16 Friday

17 Saturday

18 Sunday

> Those who don't believe in magic will never find it.
>
> *Roald Dahl*

Week 52

Welcome to Week 52.

How did you get on? Did you complete a goal related to the passengers on the bus task? Take a moment to reflect on your experience. Were your behaviours this week generally value consistent or value inconsistent?

Record some values and goals that are important to you and which you can try to complete in the next week.

December 2022

Ending the Year

That's the end of the year! Congratulations and well done for bringing your values and goals centre stage; we hope that you are living a fuller life as a result of engaging with this diary. And now, let us give you our take home message:

Anything worth doing in life is likely to bring with it a shedload of discomfort. As a good rule of thumb, the more something matters, the more challenge, uncertainty and angst we will feel. Many people respond to these things by staying in their comfort zone. However, you don't have to. You can move out of that comfort zone and learn for yourself that that's where the magic of life happens.

How do we do this? First, we need to decide what we really want to do and how we want to do it. If you know this already then great, but if you're unsure then a good place to start is by reviewing your values and writing some goals related to them. Set yourself some short-term targets and some that are harder or more challenging.

Whatever your goals, try to move yourself out of your comfort zone – but expect a host of unwanted thoughts and feelings to pop up on the way. When they come along remember to embrace them willingly, defuse unhelpful thoughts, maintain contact with the present moment and hold your self-stories lightly.

We hope you've found our year together useful, and we wish you the best of luck going forward.

Nic and Freddy

Where the magic happens...

Your Comfort Zone

December 2022 Week 52

Summary goal for the week

19 Monday

20 Tuesday

21 Wednesday

December 2022 Week 52

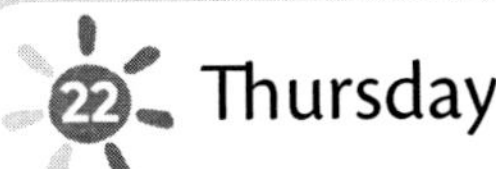

Thursday

Friday

Saturday

Sunday

Others have seen what is and asked why. I have seen what could be and asked why not.

Pablo Picasso

December 2022 Week 1

Summary goal for the week

26 Monday

27 Tuesday

28 Wednesday

December 2022/January 2023 Week 

Thursday

Friday

Saturday

Sunday

When you have exhausted all your possibilities, remember this: you haven't.

Thomas Edison

Space for general reflection

Use this space to record the ups and downs of the past few weeks. You may also want to write down what you have learned about yourself and the nature of life.

Goal Bank

Goal Bank

About Nic and Freddy

Dr Nic Hooper

Nic is an expert in clinical psychology and a Senior Lecturer in Psychology at the University of the West of England in Bristol. He has authored many scientific articles, book chapters and books including *The Research Journey of Acceptance and Commitment Therapy* and *The Unbreakable Student*. Nic is a co-director of Connect (which is an organisation that offers a psychological wellbeing curriculum for primary school children) and for two years he sat on the board of the Association for Contextual Behavioral Science (ACBS), the 8,000-member organization that oversees a lot of ACT related work. He is the co-author of *The Acceptance and Commitment Therapy (ACT) Journal*.

Dr Freddy Jackson Brown

Freddy is an HCPC (Health and Care Professions Council) registered chartered clinical psychologist with 20 years' experience working with children and families in the NHS. His practice is child centred and focuses on helping individuals learn the communication and everyday living skills needed to live a more independent and fulfilling life. He has published a range of peer reviewed articles, book chapters and books including *When Young People with Intellectual Disabilities and Autism Hit Puberty* and *ACT for Dummies*. His interests include child development, language and communication, challenging behaviour, staff systems, emotional literacy and supervision. He is the co-author of *The Acceptance and Commitment Therapy (ACT) Journal*.